Sophie Ryder New Work

Curled up 2009
Etching with chine collé, edition of 70
42 x 59
Donated by the artist to raise funds for the Victoria Art Gallery

The Eloquence of the Fragment

Jonathan Benington

Over the last five or six years there has been a marked shift in Sophie Ryder's work, away from the outer world of human and animal interaction towards an inner world of thoughts, dreams and spirituality. The vertical, physically active poses she once favoured for her figures have now on the whole been replaced by horizontal, reflective ones. Through the 1990s she made many sculptural groups involving a cast of four or more characters. These have now all but vanished, alongside the ancillary preoccupation with family relationships in which a minotaur usually acted as consort to the 'lady-hare' (the two are partnered again in the recent *Hugging*, but the embrace is comforting rather than sexual). Even the lady-hare has not remained immune to change, evolving from a semi-human figure based on Ryder's own body, with the large ears standing proxy for a mane of hair, into a woman wearing a hare mask that covers the entire head, down to the shoulders. These shifts in external form have also been accompanied by new concerns, both artistic and personal, and as the artist moves into her mid- forties, there is a strong feeling of confidence and maturity about the work. What it may lack in physical dynamism, it more than makes up for in terms of thought-provoking content, rendered very directly, without technical frills or sentimental whimsy.

Since 2005, it seems to me that Ryder has reverted to the roots of her own sculptural practice, if not to the roots of sculpture *per se*, in the sense that the starting point for her new body of work has been a seemingly insatiable curiosity for living tissue, encompassing its feel, texture and pulse, and how it moves from softness to tense firmness in different situations. Like a nineteenth-century art student instructed to work from plaster casts (in the early 1980s Ryder had been an appreciative habitué of the cast corridor at the Royal Academy Schools), she made a series of finely drawn and carefully observed studies of eyes, ears, mouths, hands and feet, treating each as a complete form in its own right. Hands in particular seemed to inspire her, as I first realised in 2001 when sharing a cab in London with the artist and her husband Harry. She was so struck by my long and, as she mistakenly assumed, piano-playing fingers, that she grabbed my hand and held it aloft for our fellow passengers to see. Five years later, on a visit to Ryder's studio, I could see the results of her instinctive need to assimilate plastic form emerging as a substantial body of new work: those small pencil drawings had morphed into huge wire drawings and wire sculptures, with the intermediate scale catered for by a number of plaster maquettes.

The trail of finished or half finished 'body parts' even extended into the adjoining landscape, where one of the wire drawings of an eye was suspended between two poles, dramatically silhouetted against the blue sky and giving new meaning to the phrase 'drawing the eye'. Two dimensional works also littered the bungalow that was once the family home and now did duty as a drawing studio. The creative outpouring I was witnessing was both impressive and inspiring, all the more so considering the vast majority of assembled works were one-offs rather than multiples (in the case of an intractable material such as wire, which is tough but lacking in volume, the making process is one of grueling, repetitive manual labour). I fell to wondering what had inspired this new direction – above and beyond the obvious anatomical curiosity –, and secondly what was the link between the partial figures (the physical extremities and orifices) and the complete ones that were being nurtured into existence at the same time?

While there are many precedents, both ancient and modern, for making figures on a massive scale, from Abu Simbel and the *Great Sphinx* of Giza to Leshan's *Colossal Buddha* and New York's *Statue of Liberty*, comparatively few sculptors have set themselves the task of creating complete works using individual components of the body. The giant marble hands, feet and heads that can be seen in the Capitoline Museum, for example, are tantalising fragments

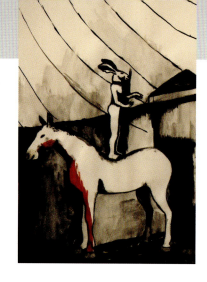

Sketchbook drawing, hare on horse

of once complete, oversize figures that towered above their ant-like spectators, striking them with awe and wonder. Such survivors of ancient civilisations fire our contemporary imaginations, making us want to fill in the missing pieces of the jigsaw. Indeed, the impulse to reconnect the part into a larger whole is so strong that we tend to overlook the fact that the fragment has its own formal and expressive integrity: the act of violence or structural weakness that made it a fragment in the first place has become an integral part of its history, a stage on from the processes of gestation, handling and weathering. The first artist who fully grasped the sufficiency of the part and allowed it to inform his own sculptural practice was Auguste Rodin, whose *The Mighty Hand* dating from about 1880 was just one of many works he made featuring a hand or a pair of hands detached from the body. Such radical (for the time) cropping of the human form endowed the hand with its own meaning, allowing its expressive capability to be fully appreciated for the first time.

Sophie Ryder likewise exploits hands as indicators both of feeling and personality. Her hand sculptures have evolved their own 'body' language, from cradling, cupping and clasping to forming an encircling fist. They have also assumed titles such as *The Kiss* (showing a pair of clasped hands) that elevate them from the specificity of a sketchbook study (modelled for by one of her children) to the status of a universal metaphor implicit in the type of gesture being enacted. This is something Rodin attempted to do with his bronze of 1908, *The Cathedral*, in which two lightly touching, extended right hands formed an opening akin to the nave of a gothic church. The key to understanding both the Rodin and the Ryder is in the tactile interaction between the two forms: the extent of the zone of contact and/or overlap, the lightness or heaviness of the touch, and our ability to see it as an echo of

something else – be it a place of worship, or an act of physical intimacy. The titles coax us to take a metaphorical journey, but even without the titles, surely we ought to be able to interpret the language of touch, given that this sense is so integral to our everyday experience of the world. While the potential is certainly present in all of us, albeit embedded within our collective unconscious, as with so many things it is prone to being corrupted by the images of violence, cruelty and degradation with which the media bombards us. Ryder's hands, feet, eyes and mouths stimulate our awareness of the non-verbal channels of communication, casting us in the role of receiver vis-à-vis the work's function as large-scale transmitter.

Ryder's 'complete' figures, by which I mean the kneeling, sitting, lying and curled-up figures wearing hare masks, are based on her own body, the masks lending them a timeless anonymity that is free from the connotations of portraiture associated with the depiction of the face (the effect is similar to that of the animal masks worn by Aztec deities such as Quetzalcoatl). Emerging at the same time as the pieces devoted to facial features and physical extremities, the un-cropped figures have benefited from the intensity of focus required to make an eye, an ear or a foot.

It is noticeable that the hands and feet of the masked figures have become chunkier and more prominent, and when placed in close proximity (as they usually are) they convey a striking monumentality. The artist's skilful handling of her material ensures that such massive forms do not detract from the almost Zen-like stillness that envelopes these figures. At the same time the closed eyes and coiled, S-shaped poses that the figures typically adopt are suggestive of a state of being that is 'in touch' – literally as well as metaphorically – with its inner self. This internalising of the feminine, treating her as a conceptual being rather than an overtly sensual one laid out for the viewer's delectation, provides a 21st-century update on the traditional subject of the reclining nude (Henry Moore's recumbent figures of the 1920s/'30s have a similar massiveness but still meet our gaze, notwithstanding their mask-like faces). One could even argue that Ryder has created a new genre – that of the reflecting nude.

Introspective 2003
Wire, life-size

The interest in exploring more meditative poses can be traced back to two installation pieces, *Lady-Hares in a Forest* of 1999 and *Introspective* of 2003. Whereas the former comprised five standing figures amongst trees, the latter was limited to four life-size figures variously kneeling, bending, squatting and standing, as if depicting four states of mind pertaining to the same individual (the events of nine eleven were much in Ryder's mind when creating this piece). In the intervening period, the crouched, protective pose has been extracted and developed further, face down and face up as well as on its side, and now with the added complexity of slicing the figure vertically into sections (the clean-ness of the cuts recalling Damien Hirst rather than Henry Moore). Dividing the figure into component parts in this way could easily lead to a loss of focus, but Ryder avoids this by adopting a stratagem already perfected in her wire drawings of hands and eyes: she employs a series of concave curves to create encircling forms. These direct our attention towards the core of the piece, rooting us visually and mentally at its centre of gravity and avoiding any risk of distraction in the surrounding space.

The gaps separating the constituent parts of the divided figures are never so wide that we cannot bridge them with our inner eye, our imagination (just as our perception of their wire mesh bodies alternates between openness and solidity). And with the largest of the figures we can even go a step further and physically enter the sculptures using the gaps as points of access; in the case of *Kneeling* 2006, the viewer can sit down inside the sculpture, the positioning of the 'seat' being such that it leads to an encounter with a smaller crouching figure attached to the inner wall of the piece. Thus we can quite literally penetrate the inner state personified by the crouching or foetal figure, taking shelter *inside* its sheltering pose. Far from this work being exclusive or excluding, the artist breaks down the invisible barrier that exists between the viewer and the viewed, affording us privileged access to these most private of moments so that we can explore them with our eyes, minds and bodies. The physical journey embarked upon by the spectator parallels the artist's mental journey, leading us towards a still point, a safe place where calm reflection provides an encouragingly robust alternative to the 'noise', insanity and fear of the world we live in.

Study for large Curled Up, wire 2008-9

Colour plates

Since childhood, Sophie Ryder has felt driven to make multiple versions of the same subject, using a range of different media and working to a variety of scales, from the tiny to the monumental. Her only motivation is one of perfectionism – having made something once, she wants to make it again, only better. It is intended that this visual essay should prove revealing of Ryder's working methods, her versatility and her insistent investigations of both space and scale.

Blue Eye 2007
Wire drawing
Annealed wire
365 x 548

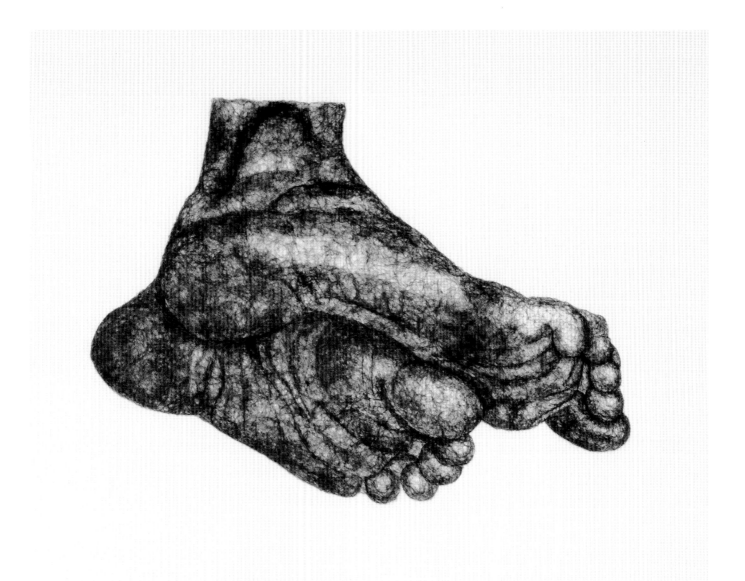

Nell's Feet 2007
Wire drawing
Annealed wire
160 x 200

The Kiss 2008
Annealed wire
200 x 203 x 75

Open Hand with Figure 2007
Plaster
101 x 170 x 88

Sitting Lady-Hare 2003
Wall piece
Bronze, edition of 9
30 x 16 x 9

Minotaur and Lady-Hare Torsos 2000
Galvanised wire
Each 287 x 305 x 120

Curled up Figure 2004
Bronze, edition of 9
18 x 33 x 30

Paint Pots 2003
Bronze, edition of 9
214 x 232 x 80

Hugging 2008
Plaster for bronze
69 x 30 x 30

Feeding 2009
Plaster for bronze
27 x 33 x 13

Hugging 2008
Bronze, edition of 9
69 x 30 x 30

Feeding 2009
Bronze, edition of 12
27 x 33 x 13

Sitting 2009
Charcoal on board
30 x 23

Reclining Figure looking back 2009
Charcoal on board
23 x 30

Girl with arms up (back) 2009
Charcoal on board
30 x 23

Girl with arms up (left) 2009
Charcoal on board
30 x 23

Girl with Arms up (front) 2009
Charcoal on board
30 x 23

Hugging 2008
Charcoal and pastel on board
122 x 91

Girl leaning on Horse 2009
Charcoal on board
122 x 91

Girl on Bear 2009
Charcoal on board
122 x 91

Eye 2007
Tapestry
60 x 80

Exhibited but not illustrated

All measurements in centimetres, height by width, followed where applicable by depth

Wire, plaster and bronze:

Open Hand II 2008
Wire drawing
Annealed wire; 122 x 279

Bending Figure I
Bending Figure II
Bending Figure III
Wire drawings
Annealed wire
208 x155; 160 x 127; 165 x 122

Girl behaving like a Dog 2007
Plaster; 14 x 35 x 20

Upside down kneeling 2007
Plaster; 28 x 66 x 28

Paint Pots Maquette 2004
Bronze, edition of 9; 51 x 51 x 20

Introspective 2003
Bronze, edition of 9
Standing figure 68 x 17 x 18
Crouching figure 21 x 39 x 17
Kneeling figure 37 x 23 x 16
Bending figure 35 x 26 x 17

Drawings and tapestries:

Feeding 2009
Charcoal on board; 23 x 30

Dancing 2009
Charcoal on board; 23 x 30

Dancing II 2009
Charcoal on board; 23 x 30

Dancing III 2009
Charcoal on board; 23 x 30

Dancing IV 2009
Charcoal on board; 23 x 30

Dancing V 2009
Charcoal on board; 23 x 30

Feeding 2009
Charcoal on board; 122 x 91

Girl on Horse with Bird 2009
Charcoal on board; 122 x 91

Girl with Arms up (right) 2009
Charcoal on board; 23 x 30

Couple dancing 2009
Charcoal on board; 23 x 30

Girl with Dog on Shoulder 2009
Charcoal on board; 23 x 30

Open Hand with Figure 2008
Charcoal on Corri board; 122 x 91

Curled up Figure 2007
Charcoal and pastel on Corri board;
122 x 91

Upside down kneeling 2007
Charcoal on Corri board; 122 x 91

Girl behaving like a Dog 2007
Charcoal on Corri board; 122 x 91

Curled up 2005
Tapestry; 54 x 54

Prints:

Girl leaning on Horse 2009
Etching with chine collé, edition of 50;
40 x 31

Girl on Bear 2009
Etching with chine collé, edition of 50;
40 x 31

Girl on Horse 2009
Etching with chine collé, edition of 50;
40 x 31

Sophie Ryder

1963 Born London

1980 Foundation Course, Kingston Polytechnic

1981-4 Royal Academy Schools

Exhibitions

1984 Christie's Inaugural Pick of the Graduates Interim Art London

1985 Henley Festival Gallery 24, Harry Scott & Sophie Ryder

1986 Yorkshire Sculpture Park

Laing Art Gallery, Newcastle-upon-Tyne

Photographers Gallery, London

1987 Edward Totah Gallery, London

Louise Hallet Gallery, London

Salisbury Cathedral

Courcoux & Courcoux Gallery, Salisbury

1988 Plymouth City Museum

St Paul's Gallery, Leeds

Courcoux & Courcoux Gallery, Salisbury

Glasgow Garden Festival

Cleveland Gallery, Middlesborough

Berkeley Square Gallery, London

Chilford Hall Press, Cambridge

Oxford Gallery, Oxford

1989 Henley Festival

Berkeley Square Gallery, London

1990 Newport City Museum & Art Gallery, Newport, Gwent

Courcoux & Courcoux Gallery, Salisbury

Glasgow Print Studio

1991 Yorkshire Sculpture Park

Hannah Peschar Gallery

1992 Art at Milton Keynes

Millfield 20th Century Sculpture Exhibition, Millfield School

Women Artists – Critics Choice, Bruton Street Gallery, London

Young British Art, Arhus Festival, Denmark

Bruton Gallery, Bath

Courcoux & Courcoux Gallery, Salisbury

Plymouth City Museum

Mall Galleries, London

1993 Oxford Gallery, Oxford

Art in the City, London

Bury St Edmunds Art Gallery, Suffolk

Kilkenny Arts Week, Eire

1994 Winchester Cathedral

Red House Museum & Gardens, Christchurch, Dorset

The Allen Gallery Alton, Hampshire

Sculpture at Goodwood

Artbus, Fife

Berkeley Square Gallery, London

1995 Berkeley Square Gallery, London

1996 Belloc Lowndes Gallery, Chicago

Chelsea Harbour, London

1997 O'Hara Gallery, New York

Cheltenham Art Gallery & Museum and Town Centre

Manchester Academy

Wimpole Hall, Cambridge

The Scottish Gallery, Edinburgh

Berkeley Square Gallery, London

Sotheby's London

1998 Vancouver Sculpture Festival

Courcoux & Courcoux Gallery, Salisbury

1999 Victoria Art Gallery, Bath and city

Shape of the Century – 100 years of British Sculpture, Salisbury and Canary Wharf, London

Den Haag Sculptuur, The Hague, Holland

Cartwright Hall Art Gallery, Bradford, Temple to the 200 Rabbits Installation

Berkeley Square Gallery, London

2000 Odapark, Venray, Holland

Veranneman Foundation, Belgium

Courcoux & Courcoux Gallery, Salisbury

Buschlen Mowatt Galleries, Vancouver

2001	Galerie de Bellefeuille,Quebec
	Kirkland International Outdoor Sculpture Exhibition, Washington
	Eigsé Carlow Arts Festival, Eire
	Den Haag Sculptuur, The Hague, Holland
	Berkeley Square Gallery, London
2002	Metropole Galleries, Folkestone, Kent
	Courcoux & Courcoux Gallery, Salisbury
	Pierrepont Fine Art, Oxford
2003	Newbury Spring Festival
	Berkeley Square Gallery, London
2004	Victoria Art Gallery, Bath Introspective, installation
	Vancouver Biennale
	Sculpture in the Park, Ackley Heads, Durham
	Imago Gallery, Palm Desert, California, USA
	Storey Gallery and Lancaster Town Centre
2005	Vancouver Biennale
	Solomon Gallery, Dublin
	Canary Wharf, London
2006	Royal Hibernian Academy, Dublin
	Atkinson Gallery, Millfield School

2007	Imago Galleries, Palm Desert, USA
	Frederick Meijer Gardens & Sculpture Park, Grand Rapids, USA
	Blickachsen 6 Bad Homburg, Frankfurt
2008-9	The Yorkshire Sculpture Park West Bretton,Wakefield
2009	Victoria Gallery, Bath and city

Artist in residence

1986	Yorkshire Sculpture Park
	Grizedale Forest, Cumbria
1987	Salisbury Cathedral
1988	Forest of Dean, Gloucestershire
1993	Kilkenny, Eire
1996	Boulogne, France
1997	Cheltenham Art Gallery, Cleeve School, Cheltenham
	Cheekwood Sculpture Park, Nashville, Tennessee
2000	Vancouver Sculpture Festival
2003	Newbury Spring Festival

Lectures and teaching

Sheffield Art College
Loughborough Polytechnic
Ikon Gallery Birmingham
Cheshire Art Teachers Conference
Staffordshire Art Teachers Conference
Jesus College, University of Cambridge

Cheltenham Art Gallery & Museum
Victoria Art Gallery, Bath
Kirkland International Outdoor Sculpture Exhibition Washington
Mary Hare School, Newbury
Victoria Art Gallery, Bath
Frederick Meijer Gardens & Sculpture park, Grand Rapids, USA
Oxbow School of Art, Saugatuck, Michigan, USA

Public and corporate collections

Yorkshire Sculpture Park, Newport City Museum & Art Gallery, Barings Bank, De Beers Collection, Gerrard & National Bank, New Hall College, Cambridge, Conoco Ltd, Butler Gallery Collection, Kilkenny, Eire, The Private Bank and Trust Company Ltd, The National Trust, Cheltenham Art Gallery & Museum, Cheltenham Borough Council, Cheekwood Museum of Art, Nashville, Tennessee, Victoria Art Gallery, Bath, Robert and Mary Montgomery Armory Arts Center, Palm Beach, Florida, Ballantrae Park Dublin, Ohio, USA, Frensham Heights School, Folkstone Town, Frederick Meijer Gardens & Sculpture Park, Grand Rapids, USA

Books

Jonathan Benington, Sophie Ryder, Lund Humphries, 2001

Sophie Ryder New Work

Victoria Art Gallery, Bath
City centre and Bath Abbey

4 April to 10 June 2009

Published for the exhibition

Text copyright © Jonathan Benington and
Bath & North East Somerset Council, 2009

All images copyright © Sophie Ryder
and Harry Scott

Photography by Harry Scott
Design: www.ninepoint.co.uk
print: www.emtone.co.uk

Victoria Art Gallery
By Pulteney Bridge
Bath BA2 4AT

01225 477244
www.victoriagal.org.uk
victoria_enquiries@bathnes.gov.uk

Sponsored by
The Framing Workshop